My Mother Did Not Tell Stories

My Mother Did Not Tell Stories

poems by Laurie Kruk

DEMETER

DEMETER PRESS, BRADFORD, ONTARIO

Published by:
Demeter Press
140 Holland Street West
P. O. Box 13022
Bradford, ON L3Z 2Y5
Tel: (905) 775-9089
Email: info@demeterpress.org
Website: www.demeterpress.org

Demeter Press logo based on Skulptur "Demeter" by Maria-Luise Bodirsky
<www.keramik-atelier.bodirsky.edu>

Printed and Bound in Canada

Library and Archives Canada Cataloguing in Publication
My mother did not tell stories / Laurie Kruk

ISBN 978-1-927335-09-3

Cataloguing data available from Library and Archives Canada.

For my mother, Betty and my daughters, Elena and Bobbie-Ann:
my support and my inspiration across the generations.

ALSO BY LAURIE KRUK

POETRY:
Loving the Alien
Theories of the World

NON-FICTION:
The Voice is the Story: Conversations with Canadian Writers of Short Fiction

Contents

Part I:
My Mother Did Not Tell Stories

First Birds

for Elena, 8 months

There are birds, flying
out of your throat
birr birr,   *birrr*   *birr*

folding diapers, I glance
at empty window
where moments before
wings whirred, beaks dipped
in seed reservoir, tapping glass, then
        flashed
back, into absence

leaving only your words
newly-winged—

You stick tiny, tenacious hands
right into the heart of things,
like my opening lips, too close
for a kiss,
touching tongue, teeth and mouth
as if to unlock
        —birr, birr birr!—
the swallow-starling fountain

of talk. Of feathers that fall
carelessly   all day
from our lips, swept up now into
nests of naming:
daughter. My daughter.
Of meanings
that float, from my mouth
to yours   *Mother,*
            your mother

            and write
            the air.

Heart Exercise

Mothers-in-process, we meet at intersections
of public and private. In the hallway
to the birthing unit, bent double, waiting
for the tidal   wave
that will throw the newest Crusoe
ashore, we grimace in recognition
of nurse-led neighbour: *Yes, you too....*
Three years later, lined up
for the After Hours Clinic, no supper, holding
crying toddlers to the breasts which no longer answer,
while childless ones behind check watches, shift loudly, we lock
eyes: *Yes.*
Or in the spring parking lot, six years on
where we must talk a daughter out of a dirty shirt before Grandma's:
pre-breasts wiggling, voice shrilling nine-year-old shame,
we avoid looking too closely as we pass
by, but smile our knowing.

Though years roll on,
you know that there is no end
to this working of the core;
even as we complete
one mothering task, hurry them along
to the next station
a late-learning muscle

is growing inside of me, taking
up more space, so that I ache
to expand—

Exasperated, one spring day, you send both,
girls seven and ten, for a walk to the corner,
and blessedly, they go.
Ten minutes, twenty, forty—you start to look
out the window, out
the door. Down the street. You
get in the car, heart hammering: *Yes, you too,*
start down the driveway, around
the corner
and their absence widens, takes shape as shadows
thicken obscenely at road edges. You want
to shout
to bovinely oblivious neighbours
watering lawns, sitting on their porches,
disturb the peace—*You, too*—

but just before you draw
the first bitter lungful up,
to wound the air with their names,
they come running down the road

ditch flowers
in their hands

Reliquary

The word pops out of my mouth,
and I tongue it again, gratefully
as I shake out the baggie, gently
and drop into my jewelry box,
her latest pale white nugget, pillow-planted.
Five years collecting calcium and hope,
grown in the dark,
traded in for loonies or twoonies now,
to bite off dreams with price tags at the mall.

Still I sugar their sleep
with dreams kept beneath my pillow,
wishes for Popularity, Beauty and Success
        yet not too soon, or too much
        for some days
        I am also the Evil Queen
        biting the green apple of envy, sealing
        up the glass coffin
        in a double burial: my youth, their future.

I drop the lid, with a thud.

But all night something shines
like coins slipped under cotton,
a shimmer on the ceiling

while the real girl, across the hall,
like her older sister,
slays dragons in her sleep.

Tomorrow, she will grin with a gap,
a jingle in her jeans.

But tonight, in sleep
I am pushing her out again,
lavender-grey, perfect, whole:

Thus believers maintain the illusion of
sainted lives, Madonna with Child:

our legends of ourselves

Made in China

When the Canadian Pacific Railway was constructed between 1881 and 1885.... Chinese were brought in from China to help build the railway. As soon as the CPR was completed, the Federal Government moved to restrict the immigration of Chinese to Canada. The first federal anti-Chinese bill was passed in 1885. It took the form of a Head tax of $50 imposed, with few exceptions, upon every person of Chinese origin entering the country. No other group was targeted in this way.

—*The Chinese Head Tax and Exclusion Act*
(Chinese Canadian National Council website)

One hundred and twenty years after,
the great-great granddaughters
of those who stayed home,
are the new princesses
of a cold foreign land
where barren royalty, aching
behind shiny castle walls
made money, went for tests, waited,
phoned, waited, wrote, begged, cried and waited
some more. Wrote China, who offered a tax
for loneliness, the equivalent
of a university degree
for this learning: to travel half-way
around the world

and find her, their lost daughter,
in an orphanage, hiding, under a spell,
lifted into their trembling arms by witches posing as nurses
behind photo-ready smiles, government-paid translators. A gift,
many gifts, exchanged hands
in one turn of the planet. And the curse
suddenly seemed lifted.

Ten days of bewilderment followed
exposing their dream to the world beyond walls
target of other eyes, so many pointing fingers like thornbushes
to prick their new parental exuberance, mothers, fathers desperate
to make tiny smiles their new mirrors
as they drag loaded strollers, camcorders
and diaper bags over the Great Wall
with the other dream-families, tracked by White tourists
who want to take their picture. Then through
the fourteen-hour "mercy flight"
to Canada, preparing bottles
in sinks of tiny toilet cubicles
the nervous smiles, fumbled love,
embarrassed diaper-changing laughter
of these oldest of newborns--

Two years later, at a suburb carved
out of CPR land, a birthday party:
the princesses—now named Madison, Emily, Hanna—
reunite, aged three and four. Their parents, bearing toys, tiny
sweaters or shoes and cell phones,
greet, hug and share their new wealth, proud with complaints.

Lines on their pale faces mark their late arrival
at this crowded station. While the girls sit in a circle
for balloon animals made out of air
by Pickles the clown, they don't yet know
their good fairy's blessing: travellers with multiple passports,
and a complicated pedigree,
wearing Disney princess nightgowns
mini-ipods (made in China),
t-shirts announcing the Year of the Rooster.
College funds already compounding nicely,
rewarded by time, like their parents, they will be
the new royalty, perhaps fluent
in two gazes, if not two tongues,
the inside-out, the outside-in—

Meanwhile, the railroads bisecting bush, tundra and muskeg
laid by their great-great-great-great uncles
are pulled up
with the new millennium, slag beds untended
to sink back into the dark like unmarked graves.
The National Dream of last century is now owned by bears or coyotes,
taken over by smalltown or reserve kids riding their parents' ATVs
wasting gas, picking up pig iron, scribbling
their names or profanities
on rock cuts blasted through lives
inside-out of this country.

Good-Enough Friday

April: snow's retreat: boots are flung
off, and kids reclaim
an emptied driveway—bikes, trikes,
roller blades—riding up and down
this winter-wrinkled island of return,
shrieking with every downward glide,
air newly-worn in naked hair.

And on the City news that night:
story of the five-year-old girl
thrown, in her snowsuit, from a bridge over the DVP*
by her deranged father, joint-custody weekend swap,
suicide note taunting the mother's answering machine.
More heavily, he followed
to meet the final answer of asphalt
while commuters roared past
two ragged bundles
and some braked for lives unknown,
caught between stations.

Though broken, the girl survived
to wake in hospital,
her small body less dense,
less married to gravity,

and the updrafts of anonymous cars—
angels of engines—slowed her descent
to a less final embrace by earth
and all it has evolved into,
two thousand years on:
the road that cuts through our lives
—pavement my daughters marked today
with rainbow chalk—
and returns us, mostly, home.

**The Don Valley Parkway in Toronto*

Skywheel:
Niagara Falls, Canada

"Every day, one quarter of the world's freshwater
rushes down this gorge,"
our guide yells to us,
Maid of the Mist yellow-garbage-bagged tourists,
shoulder to shoulder before the roaring,
who paid for the privilege of being safely soaked.

Fifty years ago, my parents; now us, two kids in tow.
Squirming honeymooners turn into families steering strollers
bearing ice-cream-stained tots, t-shirts proclaiming I'M THE BOSS
all caught in the cycle: rolling from bus tours to souvenir shops to
   Ripley's museum—
featuring the shoes of the largest man in the world—
in a restless quest for replenishment of dreams,
or what we want the future to witness: the big
picture, larger-than-life, *Believe it or Not!*
            Like the view
promised by this gigantic rotating sun
that looks down on both American and Canadian wonders
and draws my daughters' arm-waving shrieks
as we join the ticket line parade.

But then, like the tantrumming toddler, at forty-five, I
decide to plant my feet, refusing the ride.
From a park bench, I watch while

gondola 25—my girls, their father—rises
and falls, a dozen times, shadows blotting mine
as I wave, blow kisses
at their faceless silhouettes,
one of two dozen plexiglass eggs
chasing after their descent
before the fall
away from mother, earth.

Safely grounded, I ponder my fate,
if the ride never ends:
wandering into the Casino, finally,
nothing to lose. Or at the hotel pool, going down
the slide to plunge under, then climb onto
the patio, a chair, no one there…. Somewhere near,
a child screams, my eyes fly open: fear
flips into laughter as her mother hugs her. Look up,
and they are rounding
back to me, mouthing *Mom, Mom!* Or so I think.
One more
turn over the brink,
and they glide down to earth,
are mechanically hatched
by yawning summer staff. My older
daughter is redefined, blond hair

springing with her like sunfire. Shrieks, "You missed it!"

And I nod, hug her, re-enter the circle. More families aboard,
the wheel
turns on above us
as we seek bundles of compressed meat, sticks
of melting sugar. Meanwhile Niagara continues its endless
  cleansing. Some things
you cannot wish undone.

Pierced

Lucky thirteen, her gift: vanity's wounding,
this willing supplication
at the mall, when today, two
tiny holes are shot
in her ear lobes
by the twenty-year-old clerk, smooth-faced veteran
of nose, navel, tongue piercings, who now
speaks wisely
of past piercing rashness ("I was just a kid"), while I, the Mother
retreat to the sales counter,
sign consent forms, present VISA, punch in
the numbers—

After all, a taste of pain, spot of blood or two
is the right of any grim-faced princess
grown beanstalk-tall overnight—
even though, at the moment
of sterile penetration, she   squeezes
my hand, harder   than I expected. Then laughs, letting go
to reach upward, touch
her new markings.

The ruby-red crystals
planted in her white flesh
seem to seed the crimson petals

two weeks later, that blossom and
spill   in her pyjamas,
the night of the birthday sleepover.

Doing laundry, after:
separating out for soaking (hers, mine)
these signs of what Grandma Elsie
called "our Monthlies," I will plunge
suddenly aged hands
into cold cold water,
pierced by a new chill,

harder   than I expected

"MAW!"

Once again, it catches me—that open-
mouthed howl, wounded whelp yelp,
coming from the new giantess in torn jeans:
"Maw, there's no more milk in the fridge!"

Like a baby bird's endlessly-spread beak,
like the enveloping cloud before the thunder,
like the infant's powerful latch
on the swollen, milk-leaking nipple:
Maw—once her precious first word,
dropped syllable-jewel, swallowed by greedy ears:
my child names me her mother, I
must be one—

No longer "Mommy" or "Mom," "Maw"
now signals my turn to step back, to hover
off-stage, in the wings, offer
ignored warnings, crumbs of wisdom
old songs chanted by my mother, and hers:
Whatever doesn't kill you, makes you strong—
or was that Nietzsche's Maw?
My turn to be
dark reflection, jealous queen, evil step-mother
who lures innocents into the woods,
then leaves them there, hungry and cold

to be led to the hidden castle by talking birds
where the prince must be woken with a kiss,
or the ogre stomped on
with size ten loafers.

My turn to feel myself grasping
with bony fingers
at her new-fleshed arm; slim, shrugging shoulder
("Oh, Maw"—)
which makes me suddenly so much older
than I—opened, newly-raw—
ever thought I was, or
could be.

Scratching Tree

First, you are Mama Bear:
hiding, enclosing
nursing and holding
in the dark den of early motherhood
where you turn day into night, carry her
in the silvery-black, tracing the moon's circle:
where she is you, inside-out.

A dozen years later
she is looking you in the eye, wearing
your shoes and taking your credit card.

The young she-bear is now wandering   on her own,
digging with her new claws
claiming her own hunting grounds
preparing to make her first den

                                        and today, you are the pine

that she reaches up to scratch, to carve
deep grooved lines
into pale bark
that measure the extent of her full reach
leaving you marked and silvered
outside-in:

missing the cub you carried close

but breathless
at this newest wildlife sighting.

Between Women

> "What rule of legality and self-interest, in societies of a backward or archaic type, compels the gift that has been received to be obligatorily reciprocated? What power resides in the object given that causes its recipient to pay it back?"
>
> —Marcel Mauss, *The Gift: The Form and Reason for Exchange in Archaic Societies* (1950, trans. 1954), 4

It slips
through my fingers, floats
on my exhaling breath:
sinuous hank of pink and blue silk
she gave me, age thirteen,
Mother's Day. Lifted in the breeze
blowing round my neck, catching in my lips
as I turn to say good-bye,
going to another conference: *See you in a few days.*
All weekend, I wear it, an invisible badge
at my throat
lightest of reminders,
need to thank and be thanked,
give, and be gifted
endlessly, between generations, between
women. Another woman admires, ritual courtesy, like a
step in a dance—*I like your scarf*—

and I step forward, in time: *Yes, my daughter gave it to me.*

Like my mother, her grandmother, with her handwritten
Birthday Letters to the grandchildren, who move up, year
by year, from gifts of crayons, colouring books, Barbie dolls
and talking animals
earrings and I-pods, by-passing the written wrapping
for the golden treasure. Later, she will ask,
"Did they read it?"
and I am tugged, two ways, writing their answers
on the air of their absence: *"Yes, of course—they love
your letters"*—

The scarf my daughter bought
with the allowance we gave her,
is almost the twin of one my mother, years before,
gave me, laughable vestmental redundancy,
and I am the woman of two blue and pink scarves,
looking back, looking forward
repeating blue of our eyes, pinking of our skin
in shame, anger or love—

Mothers: the source of all giving
we think ourselves,
so why need thanking? But each day brings desire
for a new marking, written or
not, spoken or not:
when my daughter needs lunch
made in a hurry, so she can leave me,

when my mother remembers my silent husband's birthday
year after year,
when I work through the recipe, baking a cake
for her birthday, with measuring
spoons that fit together
until I pull them from the drawer, separating:

and reach for my mother's glass measuring cup
which I fill up
to the line, always
with a careful eye:
no more, no less.

Chuba
or, What She Did for It

My one-eyed father, born in Belarus eighty years ago,
lives alone, gave away his TV, collects Tim Horton
cups, plays the violin sometimes for visitors, tunes
from the Twenties and Thirties: "*the Breeze and I/*
are saying with a sigh / that you no longer care for me...."
His past is in basement storage—my divorced parents' wedding china,
our dozen growing-up albums, Baba's Russian money. Except for
  the coat
he brought to show his granddaughters, one visit: still
hanging in my hall closet, five years later.

> Lifting it down, my wrists tremble: *chuba,** Baba's prized
> possession, made entirely of astrakhan, black
> whorled lamb's wool, old world
> elegance and warmth, named for the city
> on the Volga on the other side
> of her life.

Born Julienna in Belarus, 1904, she was a half-starved orphan
sleeping on the floor of her brother's pantry. Then Mikhail took her,
promising Canada. Left her behind, big-bellied but dry-eyed.
This coat proclaims a woman of substance
who bravely shouldered life's winters,
cold as Kirkland Lake in February, nineteen-thirties
where her eight-year-absent husband called her,

sending the ticket for her and Nicky, a weak-eyed child
whose first English word, *orange,* would be a gift
from foreigners.

With a border-guard christening,
Helen found herself in a shack outside city limits
fighting black-flies, fear of bears, blazing
heat or four feet of snow, take your pick,
where she cooked, cleaned, raised her son
pushed back the bush for a few rows
of mouldy beets, onions, potatoes
and watched her husband gamble away
their savings, playing fiddle at weddings
or drunken parties for Polacks and Ruskis,
pink mining stock papers Nicky's inheritance
carefully folded in cigar boxes. Never cashed. A man
handy with underground explosives, he kept
all his fingers. Provider? Mostly
of a joke or a fiddle-song,
or the leather-belt strapping
of my father's thin legs, for reading *Little Lulu* or *Superman,*
instead of digging out stones, beating back weeds,
or lining up, shivering, at the mine—

But before she could wear the coat, Helen needed

the protection of another man's name, shielding her
  reputation
in the escape from Mike and the Mile of Gold
to the border-city of the fifties where the future was FORD,
  Chrysler, GM—
When Nick was sixteen, needing glasses, she stood,
  babushka'd* head unbowed
in a stuffy courtroom, oblivious to the label of *adultress*
as she traded in the gambler
for gentle Emil, factory janitor who spent Saturdays
tracing his fate to the bottom of a Seagrams bottle.
Taking the six a.m. bus downtown to clean offices at Ford,
she could peer in the glass Aladdin caves of capitalism,
recalling the *kulak** who denied her a deed
on her dowry, her husband's abandoned farm.
After years of cleaning offices, cooking in diners, taking
in boarders, planting fruit trees, tomatoes, beets, in her tiny
war-time garden beside the tracks, at sixty, she found
her own V-Day:

walking into the downtown furrier's, *Lazares of Windsor*,
pointing to the window, *yes, that one*—
to put it all there, trembling, on the counter
pink bills rolled with elastic bands
which the clerk quickly wiped with his hanky,
before counting. Then grunting, lifted it down, her *chuba*:
which she wore home, on the rush-hour bus, apron
  underneath
a pelt as thick as the black bear's shot in her garden, never
  feeling

its weight or the glare
of strangers grinning, trading glances, with whispers
for the *babushka*'s regal folds
in which she sat
as if ermine-encircled.

In her *chuba*, said my father, "she felt like the queen.
Well, who could wear anything
like that, anymore?" Eyes dried, he slipped his glasses
back on, to peer at the note I had found folded in one pocket,
preparing to bestow it
on the Sally Ann
this Fall:

mixture of Cyrillic
and English, capitals and lower-case.
"For GRANDutter," it said. "SOME day."

**chuba: fur coat (Russian)*
**babushka: grandmother (Russian), dim. of baba: woman. Also an old woman's headscarf.*
**kulak: wealthy Russian peasant (Russian)*

my mother did not tell stories

My mother did not tell stories—
instead, passed around our sticky kitchen table
warnings, worries, laments, teatime croonings,
that diluted childhood, muted its paintbox primary
with shadings and greys from the dark pages
of adult discouragement. *Being a man is hard work—*
don't ask your brother to dry the dishes.
Or, *My father never wanted us—the CCF took up his whole heart.*
About Grandma Elsie, dead when I closed the first circle of seasons,
My mother kept running away, but her Irish relations could only afford
to send her home. To "your husband." I was never so happy
as when they called after me, in Belfast, "Hey Canada!" Felt like a
comic-book heroine,
my tits turned pointy as maple leaves.

Our growing-up years
were not nourished by stories built around survival,
but hard crusts left over from times of stubbornness,
just enough to start a life on. Charlie and Elsie's bitter marital loaf
the proverbs of worry nibbled by my mother, sister, five grandkids.
Like a photo of Charlie's White Rose Gas Station, forties, Windsor,
where they all
slept in the back room, wearing the reek
of engine oil, spilled gasoline like a caste mark.
Selling out, Charlie went on the Line at Chrysler.

Working overtime at the Top Hat Grill, Elsie became radiantly tragic
hoping each night to be taken away
by a sensitive post-war millionaire, won by her smile
and careful way placing the coffee cups,
not a drop lost. Later, when my mother was engaged,
Elsie's rocking chair blessing: *Men have all the power, but*
they don't know it, unless we let them. Don't let him. Cradling
her saucer of cold tea
like a still-born. Five years later, ballooned by the illness gnawing
at her bowels, Elsie floated over the Atlantic in morphine dreams,
before
the landlady phoned
and they carried her back, terminally in arrears. Murmuring to the
V.O.N. *Mother,*
Mother—may I please come home, now?

My father did not tell stories:
Baba's memories, half-buried in Russian,
were too radioactive to unearth, like Chernobyl's ashy soil,
not far from where he was born. Too much old world pain waved
away—
dystentery, orphans, typhus,
greedy landlords, rotten potatoes, stolen land, emigration—
why drag it over the ocean?
So she muttered, half in English

and he would nod, sinking in his chair, retired teacher
recalling the mining town he was raised in, the ungentle man they left behind
for a new start in the border city, new father, school for Nick in Detroit,
subsiding into silence after two helpings of her cherry pie.
Along with ten dollar bills, folded into our sticky palms like crushed moths
Baba provided these free lessons:

Don't trust no-bahdee.
Look after yu-self.
Keep yur kitchen clean,
Yu money inside an old shoe.
Men, yu don't need.
Die, yu owe nuthin to no-bahdee.

Although Baba lived to one hundred, burying three husbands,
her triumph never quite equaled the loss—
moving, marrying, leaving, forgetting, burying—
the stories were lost to her rocking-chair's rhythm, grooves
worn into the floor while we waited
to turn on the TV, or escape to boys with cars. Only when we were waving
good-bye, from the parking lot of the Home
to her balcony watch
did the old words suddenly flow
from her lips: curses or thanks,
we'll never know.

Part II:
River Valley Poems

Dump Day

Youse from round 'ere?
Drop off on da right, den
the man in the *Coors Light* cap says,
Sunday morning, jotting down plate numbers,
while his half-wolf sniffs
our suspiciously-clean tires:
the Anglos who bought Old Hector's Camp last fall.

We roll up to the ridge:
July woods wrapped in summer haze
and layers of plastic—garbage and grocery bags, spilling
reeking debris: hill to hill panorama
of heat-shimmering melting decay,
puzzle pieces of discarded lives:
old chairs, broken toilets, boxes, settees
carpet ends, toys, books, bike wheels
mattresses, smashed dishes, undefined rubbish,
all waiting in the sun for time's slow erasure
—or the bulldozer, whichever comes first.

Stepping down from the van, I see
blue-black necklace of bear poop
dropped on the ground like a rosary.
Though not church-goers, we believe in the sanctity
of possession, of property: we too

are tax-payers, we too
have a right to drive in,
a mile out of town,
up to the edge of the half-road   to throw
our tidy Glad bags
as far as possible into this corner
of unclaimed bush,
its thinning wall of trees, birch and pine
now hung with new plastic leaves,
drowning in a malodorous sea.
        To the kids, it quickly becomes a sport,
        like caber toss or stone skipping:
        how many times will it bounce?
        How many birds raise a fuss?
        How far can it travel from us?
        How quickly can we duck away,
        dodge the rising stink   of ownership?

The dump man patrols, jingling
like a reverse Santa in his bear bells.

As cars or trucks pull up, we quickly learn
to avert our gaze: it's not polite to look
too closely
at your neighbour's garbage. Smile and nod vaguely
as the Sunday ritual is completed
with a heave, a grunt, a *Tabernac'*.

Sin or shame, the animals absolve us
for ravens, gulls and crows

bend to every offering, black or white, mocking—

As we climb back in, turn around, drive out, startling
a deer, now clearing
the gravel ridge of landfill before us,
inspiring the kids' thrilled *Holleee*—
I think:
we should feel lighter than this.

Phobophobe

I came to this place because of all
I am afraid to be afraid of:

Shadow-shifting bush that will separate, plunge
out, on dusky highways
to plant a thousand pounds, unnamed face
smack in our 60 kilometer an hour path—

Granddaddy snapping turtle that launches himself
from under our dock, lifting prehistoric beak
from under veined volcanic rock
just as we were talking of a dip—

Crossing abandoned ONR trestle when
the dog loses front paws between ties, yipes.
I seize her, read the gap, and fear
weights my ankles, turning muscles
fluid as the river glimpsed fifty feet below, surging
upward through each ragged
breath-step back—

The loudly-laughing neighbours who helped us
move the outhouse,
then start speaking quietly *en francais*,
fingers flicking like minnows,

as soon as we walk away, my campus sweater labeling me
(behind my back)
"ENGLISH": my prison ID—

The night that wraps us in unknown animal sounds: flap
of a bat?) rubbery bellow (of a bullfrog?) burrowing
of tiny claws, gnawing jaws somewhere
above, between eaves and attic,
unhurriedly munching, moving in—

Tiny wisps of succubi-dust that shadow us
May to September, original bite of
sin in paradise. Blood-sisters
feeding eggs, they drive us inside
to filter their whine through bed-covers and curses,
set up ashy altars of serpentine poison coils—

And: bear reports
casually tossed from riverbank to boat,
then recalled as night traps us
in hairy arms,
hiding in this wooden tent,
weighing
the ten-o-clock walk to the outhouse—

Unlike siren-shrieking nights in the city, where my fears
wear a TV newsman's pancake-smooth face
his mouth opening and closing
on everyday shootings, drunk drivers or war

here, lost under Argos-eyed trees
by the river that floods my dreams with dark,
I am learning to be afraid,
but in the old ways.

After-Earth: second spring

I

Told them not to buy it,
not to risk it. Take the money, invest, try the time-share
in Orlando, close to Disney World, our condo. Every kid
should see Mickey, Tinker Bell, visit Grandma,
right? That's a normal childhood.

***

Somewhere between reckless and romantic,
naively heroic, ignorantly brave
whatever passes for poetic justice
or the Seventh Circle of Hell, 21st century,
we bought land only to lose it:
call it a convergence of edges, exchange
of risks: twelve acres of bush bordering sistering rivers
named Sturgeon (for the monster fish hunted to extinction)
and Temagami (for the deep water people who left their name
misspelled on surveyor's maps) inside River Valley
first named by English bosses
still worked by French loggers, behind the wheel
of mill-bound tractor-trailers.

We paid taxes for property the river would reclaim,
and smiled over the survey that the lawyer
handed us in his office. For a year and a half,

were proud of every hummingbird buzz, beaver slap,
heron stare and deer leap
we thought we bought into being
with our ecological non-ownership
(bird-watchers, catch-and-release fishers)
although we did lock the gate,
nailed NO TRESPASSING to the dead tree inside.

But how do you share
time, or the land, fifty-fifty? Winter was our first
friend, defining and defending
the edges, frozen-sharp
of the rivers' hidden slumber
under blue unbordered skies
of January, February, March. Second spring
was the unseen mocker
as it released a swollen uprising
attacking the ice-eroded bank, undermining
our security, as land became river-bed
cabin turned boat-house, visited by geese
and ducks—then us, in canoe and hip-waders,
if only to rescue our documents, belongings
measure the daily encroachment
with cameras and head-shaking groans.
Causing us to retreat, defeated, to the city,
stare at the smiling TV weatherman and curse
his promise of late-April precipitation
and "nice weather for ducks."

II

May 7th: as he struggles into hip-waders, she and the kids
("can we swim in the yard?") waiting
in the car, beside the NO TRESPASSING tree,
he mutters, darkly, *Maybe we*
should just build an ark, already.

***

Spring, it's a dangerous time
especially after such a mother of a winter. But usually
by first weekend in May, it starts to
go down. Not this year. When they came in for a fill-up, May 13th,
and asked,
desperate, "Do you think it's over, has it crested?" I had to tell them,
No, I don't think we've seen the worst. It's not just nature
but who controls the dam, upriver, opening or closing it
to protect the lodges, float the boats, keep the Americans happy.

III

The smiling golden-haired man
in her dream last night, May 14th, said:
This is where we will dig up the road,
then the animals will come, and we'll all be free.
In response, the rivers roar, rising higher
than Niagara, arcing over the cabin in a rainbow mist
while bears, deer, wolves, rabbits, chipmunks
meet in the waves, unafraid

paws become webs
legs joining to become tails
swimming together
and there is no shore.

***

Eh—I seen the river come up over the bank
thirty years ago. I've seen people's lives
turned inside out, with no reporter to poke
a microphone at you. Tabernac'—my neighbour's
cabane, it like to float away, even, but I was there,
with my truck. I tied her to my bumper, by the porch,
and park it where the road still was. My brother come out,
tie the other side. We save her.

IV

When he came back, grim-faced, almost first weekend
of summer, he still needed the canoe.
And when he launched it on the driveway
didn't remember to meet the right side
of the flowing angel: fell
to wrestling, caught in its icy wings
but still clinging to the swamped canoe.
Mouth open in astonishment,
taking in mud and leaves with water,
he feared drowning before he realized,
hanging onto the half-dead tree,
it was a blessing he needed to ask for.

V

May 15th: Public Notice: the Ministry of Natural Resources
has posted a flood advisory, warning
all landowners or cottagers in low-lying areas
to prepare to vacate
their property until the crest is reached,
due to extreme levels of meltwater this spring. The use of floodgates
in the watershed
will be monitored closely. For more information, call—

***

End of May: and we are standing again on the land
we once called ours
the cabin still there, if leaning, crooked
where old earth was washed away.
Like recovering invalids, weak but grateful
we re-draw the edges, but tentatively:

the returned earth is placental
grassy hillocks painfully sculpted
like heads of the newly-born
hair still whorled and wet
and we too struggle to find
our first cry

Storekeeper

They're not from here, they live in the city—Anglos—but bought
the old man's Camp, where the rivers meet, two years ago—never
get flood insurance there. But great fishing. The woman, she's nice
but nervous. First time, tried out a *Bonjour, avez-vous dee* ... before
I rescued her:
What would you like, Madame? It was the end of May, raining,
said she was expecting it
to be warmer, hugging her freckled arms, small *nichons*. But she
had plenty of cash,
all right. Bought beer, wine, bread, burgers, chips, gas for generator,
barbecue starter. Was amazed at the variety of bug spray out on the
counter: Deep Woods Off to Citronella.
For bush girls who want to smell good, I said. Next time, she said,
blushing.

That summer, we saw a lot of them—though not so much the
man—because it poured
almost every day. I think they came in for a break, just get out of
the cabin, spend some money, check out the T-shirts and souvenirs:
dreamcatchers for your truck, moose antler
ashtrays for the cabin. Stuff like that sells every summer, rainy or
not: I import it cheap from the city.

Once she made the two little girls—just starting French Immersion,
she claimed—introduce themselves to me and my boy, counting

empties. *Je m'appelle Elise, Je m'appelle Sarah* … and ducked out, giggling, before I could say, *Je m'appelle Gaetan. Ca va bien?* Mom followed, face red, hugging a bottle of wine. Pierre disappeared: it was time for the Molson's delivery. The weekday regulars, who drink my cheap coffee all morning and barely buy a pack of matches—Jacques, Ferdinand, Gilbert—stopped telling pike stories. One said, *Jay-May-Pay-ellee Ferd-eee-nand. Parlee voo, Ma damm*? and slapped his knee. Silence. Then the words, they came down, hard as the raindrops drenching them on their walk back into the bush.

Fisher

Don't like it—been coming here for years,
since I could get a worm on, myself. *My* spot, beside
the turtle log, that's where the pike hid. Nobody told *me*
the old man croaked. My second-cousin or something like that.
And once, he gave me a beer, invited me into his kitchen.
Told me about his dead wife, how she died choking
on her own air. Creeped me out—'specially when he started bawling.
I laid my second-biggest on the table, ran out.

So the old man's sign was taken down last month,
and hanging there, a new name I don't know.
I ride to my usual spot, bait, and cast out,
keeping flies away with my smokes,
and then this stranger shows up, walking, waving
wearing nice boots. And says, Did I know this is
his property? Nice and polite, *tres angalis.*
My family and I will be coming here in the summer, reg-u-lar-ly.
Just like that. But I've been fishing here, this spot,
for almost fifteen years. I carved my initials
in the log, used to hang my beer off it
in a bucket to cool in the river. *Merde*—

So I told him, Mr. Stranger, my name,
said my Uncle used to live here, let me fish here, lots.
He scratched his beard at that, shuffled his boots.

I don't mind if you fish, when there's no one here—
but all I ask—don't leave any mess—broken glass,
or dead fish for us to clean up.
I shrugged *Sure*, then—*quel fou*! I still get my pike.
He stuck his hand out, and I thought he wanted
a drag, but no, he was waiting to shake on it.
So I dropped my cig, stamped it out—he didn't like that, eh.

But we shook, anyway.
Picked up my rod, my bucket and jumped
on my dirt bike, almost new—was my big brother's—
and started it up, so he backed off, staring
as I followed the old trail out, top speed, spitting
gravel all the way.

The Temagami Speaks: June

banks return, approach, greet
my gentler touch
where tree-gnawing beaver
or clam-fishing racoon
rewrite old edges

furnished again with fish
riding my pebbled pelt,
—pike, whitefish, bass
ruddy ground-cleaning suckers—
and dappled now by shadows,
I net the growing sun
a little longer   each day

the tiniest blade of underwater grass
wavers with my expanding   breath

bigger movings, soon
when shining surfaces
harbouring humans, meet mine
with roaring rainbow fires lit, doused
lit again
bleeding poison below
as they map my secret hollows, hills

aging me   into history

finally, they become late-lunged clumsy fish
who drive all before them,
—beetles, fish, frogs, geese—
churning sand into mud
calm into turbulence
above, outside, in

until they lose their skins
shout, moan or whisper
my undiscovered name

Building the Outhouse

When we first came here, we hung our name on the post,
parked our van on the gravel and started planning
the outhouse: that upright pine box
that anticipates the other (but for its two-way door)
placed length-wise in the earth, the subject's position
replacing the lord's—

We picked a scenic spot, within sight of the cabin
but downwind   the ground
neither too hard nor too wet, safe
(we thought) from spring flooding,
cut the traditional two-seater, reflecting a pioneer family's bond
of original creature comfort—or perhaps a place for the women
to escape the men   or vice versa
and whisper or plot, safely sheltered by nature—

Then dug the hole, with wood-braced walls
like a mine shaft,
though no gold or silver   is to be found at bottom,
(except maybe a lost twoonie or quarter, pants-pocket-dropped).
Now, six feet under we leave deposits of our earthly hours,
a reminder that *all flesh is grass*, or will be, in time—
The casual burial that escapes notice but, like a different
deposit, compounds over the years
of rumination and release   the morning or evening walk

where that least-familiar animal (us) is re-met in the bush,
an encounter with the knowledge of our nakedness,
the consumption of sinful fruit
day after day.

Retracing the path, we find offerings of rabbit scat, left like forgotten
          punctuation   the spiders, weaving
tapestry in the dusty forgotten top corners,
the occasional porcupine balancing, risking
a fall
for the taste of our sacred salt.

Ritual of the Mass

"To keep Composting Toilet from releasing
obnoxious odours, Mix 1 tablespoon with 8 oz. warm water. Spread evenly
over the Mass. Repeat every two weeks, or as needed."

Moving from outhouse to in,
behold the environmental miracle:
beside the sink, porcelain receptacle
saving water, shrinking waste
in box burial below
and guaranteed low stink—
which is why I am out here,
at ground level, earth's housewife, with my reluctant cup
of magic, rushed as a graverobber, unburying the toilet box
where the muck of necessity hides, beneath us,
all my family's contributions of the past season:
    I am out here
to accelerate the process of life's
forward movement, of change, of transubstantiation
greeted by a host of flies, worms and spiders,
as I lift the lid.
    Holding my breath, I sprinkle madly
    blindly
over our underground world
no longer anonymous in city sewers

joining industrially-treated sludge rivers
fed by fifty-thousand citizens
but our owned memorial, one day
 replenishing the soil,
nourishing below
a reminder of flesh's translation
through digestion and excretion
worms and maggots
emptying and repletion
heat and time
into all that is sweet and green   (and above ground).

Widowmaker

A century ago, this riverbank--
men lived with the bush, wives
and children prizes, safe miles away
by canoe, then T & N. O. Rail.* Men's lives were made
or denied by those giants
—jackpine, oak, maple, elm—
waiting for milling, cut down
by lumberjacks, dragged out
by horses, floated downstream
by logdrivers dervishing their living.
Trees they wrestled to the ground,
sometimes hitching a hollering
ride on trembling
limbs, through the splintering gold air;
unless, reckless in the sweaty hours
of bug-maddening heat,
they found their fate: one tree so mated
with another, that in their tangled
downfall, a husband
was brought to the ground,
buried by the bush. And the message carried home:
find poverty, or a new one.

2011, a new generation
of regrown, shrunken forest,

man and woman returning   like strangers
with chainsaw and propane
to this riverbank. Finding maples
half-gnawed by beaver, one threatening the cabin
too close for an easy cut,
you lift the axe, I bring the rope—
counting like a spell
we loop circles
around its centre
and lean back together
muttering *holy shit*
for the crash in the weeds
at our nervous feet: gift of laughter,
firewood.

Later, after dinner, you ride the river's last light
catching pixelated animals
in a digital trap
while I make tea, window-watching
until darkness wins:

here, when night falls
and flames grow
pushing us together
within wooden walls

a man and a woman
are necessary again:

chopping wood
keeping fires,
floating downstream on hollow boles
or staring out timbered holes,
coaxing the stove's slow fingers of heat
as night encroaches, history rewinds

and as we lie down
at the same time
we dream we are those giants

caught in a double felling.

**Temiskaming and Northern Ontario Railway, established 1902, became Ontario Northland Railway in 1946. In 2012, Premier Dalton McGuinty's move to wind down the ONR, part of the Ontario Northland Transportation Commission, led to vocal protests by Northern Ontario municipalities.*

Things that Go Thump in the Night

—middle of it, warm breath, safe under sleeping bag
and curtain of spring chorus, all night madness
of whippoorwill and peeper cries through open windows
cool riverfingers smoothing it down past midnight
comes the loud *thump thump* held breath, a heart-beat
and another *thump thump thump*
sudden scurrying, rustle. Sit up, scared
chilly and realize, my husband, me
it's not the dark out there that thumps
but the one in *here*—

Alarm, sounded by our companion animal,
not snoring dog
but white rabbit, hunched under kitchen table,
whiskers gently shifting
like an old man covertly adjusting dentures
but still lifting back feet to *thump thump thump*
while we grab flashlights, pour light through screens,
provoking a white frenzy of moths
and, ears straining, try to pierce
branch-crackle, wind hush, frog song—

There: caught
in our circle of battery power:
bristling pink and tan hairbrush

with tiny, outraged eyes
cowering under canoe rack, midnight burglar
stealing salt
off today's well-used paddles. We laugh, wake girls
pull them, blinking, to the mesh and wood rectangle
so thinly separating our worlds.

Now whether for night-walking porcupine, raccoon or bear
the watch has been set
and we have been told
as our hearts slow again, we return to sleep, dreaming
of red eyes that see in the dark
unseen trackers that pass in our sleep
things that go thump in the night.

Sign Language

Anglophones, monoglots
who salve our consciences, sending
our daughters to wade into
the other language at school,
we walk around town knowing we
are the disabled ones, single-tongued, awkwardly silent, flooded
out—

Yet the day the deaf fisherman
offered to take them, with his nine-year-old niece
up the river, we were taught a second speech,
of clownish face-making and big-hand shakings
into points, jabs and circles. He made a graceful figure-eight
with his hands, pointed up river with his paddle, grinning.
And busy as we were , closing up Camp at summers-end
the sun came out, the river sparkled
and we smiled and nodded. I said (to the niece)
"Not too far." He said, to the Uncle, making a smaller eight,
"Just for a little while,"
and went back to cleaning the cabin, gathering laundry, locking
canoes.

But both counting silently twenty minutes
(by breath, by heartbeat, by cloud drift)
and when twenty minutes had doubled, turned to an hour

the river empty and unanswering,
my husband unlocked his canoe, and muttering secret words
pushed hard, upstream, against the current.
I stopped making lunch as he rounded the point
and thought, *The river has taken my family*
and no one will hear me if
I scream—
The afternoon suddenly darkened, even the clouds' gentle unrolling,
the dog's panting became unpleasantly loud beside me in the kitchen
as the milk in their tumblers began to grow warm—

A shrilling call, from outside, that could be a jay—or child—pierced
me
and I left the cabin, sat by the biggest ant-hill, playing a game,
counting ants
in the grass—by the time I get to ten, they will be back ... or twenty
... or fifty—
Then sank into the grass, log-heavy, letting ants run
over my bare legs and arms, just a shortcut to somewhere, and
the held breath piled up in my chest,. like clouds covering the sun—
Until the first canoe scraped
sheepishly against the gravel
and my daughters were back, born into a new wide-eyed silence,
their father
just landing behind, also silent. It seemed
the apologizing niece had been entranced by each
new bend, calling up beavers or birds, and so—without a word—
we reached out, lifted them up the bank (the younger crying now),
Uncle bowing apology, arms flowing forward, open, absolving,

translated by the girl's chirping Franglais,
as they waved goodbye, paddling back downstream:
He say, the river, she beauties—
Je m'excuse, madame.

River Valley Rapture

May 21st, the day
an American Baptist pastor declared as
deferred Doomsday,
and the ascent into Heaven
for Believers; mundane disasters—earthquake, flood, famine,
or business as usual-- for the Rest of Us, below

we heard, floating up from the swamp
invisible spring peepers at our Camp
raising their tiny worship
in shrill prayerful unison:

it seemed
only the frogs
were going.

Lessons from the Rivers

i
six-twenty, wisps of wool
unknitting with each paddle stroke:
the edges of vision, margin
of mudbank holds
deep filling bowls
of a bear's tracking,
reclaiming property—*Ours*
but also *ours,*
as four-generation neighbours
warn us *en francais*

ii
skeleton of drowned fawn
half-buried in sand at the point:
discovering, two weeks later
what the vultures were after,
their claw-marks epitaphic
around duned curve of backbone,
this closed violin case

iii
standing   in water
by horizontal poplar, fallen

to the river's spring ravishment,
is a heron, awaiting frogs. Zen master,
is only tree, rooted and reflecting
until we come   too close—
dissolving into air, cloud, mirror

iv
Hwy 17, driving home:
snapping turtle on the center line,
cars whipping by tiny tailed island.
Before light, she rose from the riverbank
to deposit incipient eggs
in heat-humming gravel shoulder.
Reading the words of a dying
Canadian writer,
who follows lines of text to her last
unwritten breath,
I look up just in time.

Part III:
Drawing Circles

Boat Trip to James Bay

> "It's the great spaces that appeal.... I never have gone to the [sic] James Bay; I never go to it; I never shall. But somehow I'd feel lonely without it."
>
> —Stephen Leacock, "I'll Stay in Canada" (1936)

Post-Romantics, through the looking-glass
of a digital camera, we "White" family of four
(three passing as *Wonder Bread Enriched*)
are chasing North in October, boating
to the mouth of James Bay. Staring into the unfurling
water before us,
which we hope will open like a new-old chapter
of our daughters' heritage, five generations back
to the HBC Scots, their "country wives" and silent Cree guides.
Also on board, the original "Indians": father and daughter,
  warm-toned
children of Mumbai. Together we six ride the waves
on plank benches, girls huddling behind wind-buffering plastic
while at the bow of our speedboat, Travis,
a Moose Factory Cree in high-tops and headphones
motors us through long silent unfoldings
of brown and blue reflections. As close to the flying wake as I can be
without getting wet, I remember young Wordsworth,
travelling through the Alps in pursuit
of the Sublime, and wondering

where the boundary lay. He stopped a passing Peasant:
"Hard of belief, we questioned him again,
And all the answers which the Man return'd....
*Ended in this, that we had crossed the Alps.... I was lost as in a cloud."**

Engine-roar-wrapped, I too yearn
to burst free, into new and old. Our blue horizon never changes, just
widens   as we wait for the oracle
in the bow to divine for us,
tell us when we have arrived. But he remains twice hidden,
by rap music sybiling his eardrums, by the familiar route of a dozen
such trips
with baffled tourists who, like children, must be taught to read anew.

Abruptly, Travis points left—"Bird Sanctuary"—as a dozen Snow
Geese obediently rise
rwo ragged vees veering South, and we crane our necks, raise
cameras—
try to waken ourselves to the present,
revisited in the future, stored on home computers. The birds
disappear. The girls

yawn, while the Dads, keeping watchful silence at the back of the
boat,
check their batteries. Now Travis stands,
like Charon, piloting us further into cultural darkness
while we grow numb from unchanging blue
eyes wearied from horizon-gazing for Belugas, once
hunted to feed the fort's hunters. And finally I can't
stand it, shout *Is this James Bay? Is this it?* And taking off

his headphones, Travis nods, and waves at the left bank
far behind us
where unrelenting tamarack and spruce have disappeared, I now see
from marshy lowlands of muskeg and scrub
and mud. He cuts the engine. "*There*—" We make a long, slow arc
turning back, South, glad spray in our faces, and I tell the girls,
wind swallowing my words: We've been there now—*James Bay,*
  next to Hudson Bay,
doorstep of the Arctic. It's your history too as my daughters giggle, play
  slaphands,
and the other daughter, looking relieved, takes out her copy of
  Twilight.

While I repeat, insisting, for someone's benefit—Wordsworth's,
  Travis's, mine?—
It's your history, too.

*William Wordsworth, *The Prelude, or Growth of a Poet's Mind* (1798, 1805, 1850: 6, 520-29).

Translating the Bush

> "For seven years I had lived out of the world entirely; my person had been rendered coarse by hard work and exposure to the weather.... I was no longer fit for the world; I had lost all relish for the pursuits and pleasures which are so essential to its votaries...."
>
> —Susanna Moodie, *Roughing it in the Bush*, 476

Sometimes I dream of
a magical, middle-aged pregnancy
and wake up empty-bellied, still smiling—

Sometimes I dream of
a younger lover who takes me as I am,
and wake up beside my sleeping husband, glowing—

Sometimes I dream
I am Susanna Moodie's granddaughter
waking in our cabin-cocoon
on the riverbank where I came with my husband, in my forties
trailing daughters, rabbit, dog
crossing the rubicon (if not the Atlantic)
down a gravel, then dirt, road to where it all ends
in water. Self-named pioneers translating
between bush and town, human

and animal, awake and
dreaming. For seven bush summers
seeking peace, plenty or redemption
minus internet, phone, television
through rituals of almost-forgotten work:
chopping wood   lighting lanterns
hauling water   washing dishes
making fires   cutting paths

Seeking the lost voices
speaking almost-forgotten speech:
hiss of woodstove   spring frog chorus
summer birdchatter   fall wolf howls
winter's ice music as the river

opens   and closes
cracking, tinkling, chiming
shedding its skin

Susanna's sister* named
some of these field flowers I pick
to arrange in a green Coke bottle,
delivered by the river—Bachelor's
Buttons, Butter-and-Eggs,
Viper's Bugloss, Queen Ann's Lace—

Meanwhile, Susanna was painting butterflies
on swollen white bellies
of tree-clinging fungus
to send back to Britain,
sold as colonial curiosities—

Naming, marking, claiming:
I too scribble down interpretations
or rehearse them, in my head
as I make beds, or stand
at the sink, hands in greasy water
eyes out the window, watching the fox   pause
on our half-pasture edge, golden eyes
on mine, unrecognized, for a breath

Though not called upon, like Susanna
to bake (and burn) bread, wash shirts
with homemade soap, milk terrifying cows
or make coffee from dandelion roots,
I too am called to witness
not just the first footsteps, marking our path
not just the river's violent rebirth, spring by spring
not just my daughters' bigger ventures,
from chasing toads and butterflies
to taming chipmunks and squirrels
to riding, then resisting, the current

—kayak-girl startling the heron, its own motion, in lifting off
a letter in a language that becomes more recognizable,
every year, if still not ours—

For this is work too
earning our place here, humbly
and slowly, learning the patience
of an August cloud, spilling

unfolding in continual
growth, as my aging body
meets the river's, more
grateful every time

I am neither the first not last
namer or singer here
in any language, my Grandmothers remind me

Yet the sensation of a world, still waiting
to break through its husk,
like the memory of a lost child
stencilled in the flesh
haunts me, just as it haunted Susanna
provoked prayers to a sterner God

Her Bush was *Sublime* and *Awful*,
mine speaks a language of un-knowing
like the surf of trembling aspen or poplar
played by a passing breeze
tuning the air I breathe,
a speaking I am slowly learning to put inside me
to store up in winter's wisdom
like my Grandmothers' fruit preserves:

making use of these windfalls, neglected
lessons, unharvested plenty.

*Catherine Parr Traill, author of *The Backwoods of Canada* (1836), among many other works of colonial Canadian literature.

Weight Time

Peering out #405's fish-eye spyhole
everyday, in darkened tunnel-vision,
my father waits for the *All-Clear*
of decorously closed doors, unbroken sea
of aging blue broadloom, harbouring fallen
clouds of ten thousand
dinner hours. But ten years alone here (so he tells me)
has taught him to prepare a face
for the hallway, then the elevator: non-committal mask,
feelings retracted like claws, buttons not yet pushed
as the doors solemnly meet, closing them in,
to smile
with just the lips, revealing this:
a well-groomed elderly man, neither over-weight nor malodorous,
but aware of the space he should put around
each day's random assembly,
especially women, children, dogs.

Behind the closing, the unknown,
sometimes one, sometimes nine:
a white man, a brown woman, biting back
a fight, and their whining dog;
a couple speaking Greek, smelling of fish,
and their giggling children;
an Oma and Zaide, she muttering to his stiffly turned

back; a dwarfish, over-perfumed transvestite
making him gaze at the floor
to find
pink pumps, size ten, daisy
ankle chain.

With 22 floors, 7 units each
he calculates at least 600 people and pets
living in a vertical village
of adjacent strangers, all
piled on top of faceless neighbours
hiding behind familiar masks, hushing leashed feelings.

Bearing the weight of that compressed
silence, of stalled bodies riding the shaft
in daily communion, descent or rise,
makes his chest squeeze
in whispers of angina
as he smiles, makes a rescuing gesture
towards that other world, out there:
how hot it is, how cold, how wet,
to receive in return grateful murmurs, glances, nods
            even a cough
is enough—

Otherwise, the weight of it could kill you,
he knows

like the compounded force
of their precarious bodies, twitching synapses,

unnamed lives
plummeting into a mass basement grave

once the cord of civility
is cut.

For Three Nights Only

The man who has made a second, solitary career
out of retirement, a second bachelorhood post-divorce
is trapped   for three summer days
in this noisy house, holding two other
parents, two granddaughters, one dog. Three computers,
two video game systems, a ringing phone
for the older girl, *Oh-Em-Gee.*
As the latest reality show comes on, he carries his battery radio
into our emptied air-conditioned bedroom
where it whispers six-o-clock tragedies in his ear
like a long-distance lover. My father must have read
almost a thousand books
in these twenty-six years, spending part of every day
entering the words of
someone else. Now, he arrives with three Toronto newspapers
which he can't seem to unfold. Sits on the porch swing, halfway
between outside and in, stranger and kin, watches the street
like a traffic cop. Being on the edge
of public and private, he is free to observe
the curve of a walking women's leg, read aloud
the passing bumper sticker SPENDING THE GRANDCHILDREN'S
INHERITANCE
or count the dogs that are marshalled briskly by. He brings one
cotton shirt
with pockets for pen and notepad, a wash cloth so thin

it bleeds light as well as water
(unlike the new one I put out)
to push into the well-written lines
of his face.

The first morning, he is up
before I can make coffee, finding his way
four blocks downtown, passing dog-walkers
to take a window seat with a decaff and muffin at Tim's. For an hour
watches the cars
turn in, roll down, fill up, roll up, leave. Opens his notepad, writes
The stranger
the face, the more familiar to me.

The second, he is up
even earlier, creaking door
and car trunk, so that I run down   on the porch
in my nightgown
catch him
packing up, grinning like a truant, red-handed. "My walls miss me."

But returns to the breakfast table
for a bowl of oatmeal
to stoically serve out the duration of his dear sentence. Like the one
he is always revising, rewriting, in valedictory: *Thank you*

for your hospitality, your kindness
overwhelms me—

And so on the fourth day—*Let There Be Absence*—he leaves
the sleeping teenagers a bundle of bills
on the kitchen table,
after praising their final efforts to weigh him down with
bacon, eggs, browned leftover potatoes, strong coffee:
You feed me so well
I have to leave before there are two of me. Pointing
to his chest, pocketed notebook:
I'll write you, he promises his daughter
and does, a week later: trading white walls in solitary
for paper houses of imagined
family—*Dear Child, I miss*
you so—

The In-Laws for Christmas Dinner

What we can agree on:
That the sacred bird must be sacrificed
at three hundred and fifty degrees
of the interior sun, ruling the day
from mother-robed morning
till solstice-dusk, when man-stomachs growl,
and the wand of augury, read by three hands, declares *It's time.*
That all the trimmings are required—gravy, cranberries, homemade
   stuffing—and
Thou Shalt Not leave the table until bellies groan and spouses frown.
That family is the heart of Christmas and we'll try to "be nice,"
even to those we avoid most of the year. That dishes
 must be done, but left to the least "merry"
making soapy penitence afterwards, alone.

What we can't:
What to do with the silence between mastication, mouth-
fuls of labour shared annually by assorted personalities
crammed into Grandma's kitchen, joined
by quirks of courtship, breeding, blood. Who
to talk to, *whom* to ignore, what children can get away with
(disappearing, mid-meal, to TV?), what they can't
(eating dessert without cleaning their plate? Although Grandma *did*
buy fudge cookies just for them—).
Who has the correct memory of the last time the basement flooded,

or the middle brother tried to kill the younger with a snow shovel,
or the year the dog was run over by the neighbour, rushing to hospital
for a burst appendix or a miscarrying step-daughter.
That adolescents should be seen and not heard from,
or heard from (long-distance, collect, or email) and not seen.
That ex-wives must never, ever be mentioned,
(even with bloodcells swept with the liquor of human kindness?)
and that Grace (if remembered) must never take up
more than two cooling breaths to say
before starting in on the martyrdom of meat-
ing.

Blown Job

At the In-Laws' 40th Anniversary party
husbands and wives sit on opposite sides.
"I hear Dr. Phil has come out in favour
of marital sabbaticals," says the wife
with cherry-pink toenails. The husband
with printed-on-tuxedo tee asks
if a Research Assistant comes with it, "preferably
blonde." So five couples will be pictured, bracing
for the celebratory photo, signalling *You Are Here,*
but someone will always be cut
off, caught red-eyed or blinking. Time to cough up
for the anniversary gift, a digital
family album, on screen, clicking mercilessly
through the years, three seconds, or a breath, per memory—
kids, houses, pets, Christmas, vacations, kids' weddings—
married life, on credit or rotation.

My husband and I, a decade in
sit in the middle, unsure when
to laugh or flinch, learn or shrug. The Anniversary couple rises
leads the way
to the buffet table, she fluttering
about her diet; he, reaching, with a sigh,
for a light beer. Lingering over selections
of charred meat, rib or chicken

I tell about our pet rabbit,
who made love, yesterday
to a yellow balloon, left over
from our daughter's sixth birthday:
vibrating his tiny maleness
against yielding cornered latex
until, pressured into another dimension
            it   popped, love disappeared
and our girls collapsed, shrieking
on the rug where the rabbit sat
 red eyes staring
into nothing (we can only think) bereft
but of airy nothing—

So we make a parable
about deflated romance
while we sit and fill ourselves

till our edges threaten
either to overlap, or explode—

This is the learning, then: try to keep it
from leaking away each day,
in the slow exhalation
of lost dreams, gained space, over
-draft protection
or one quick living room detonation.
Picking through the day's feast
of needs; plunging into necessary depths of rage, then
coming back up for air

inspired by hallmarks of public coupledom,
to join occasions that spill over
their own inadequate markers
of photos, gifts and blown-out candles,
tiny flames extinguished on a sigh:

till breath do us part.

Catching the Rabbit

What is this dance in the dark
played out in uncut grass, ragweed and dandilions
behind our deck
part-way between tackle football and hide and seek?
White, sleekly furred, admirably fat, the pet
rabbit in our yard
does not know friend from foe, naked giant doe
from wolf, fox or bear,
and the formerly sun-drowsy lagomorph
nesting like a hen in his own fluffed pelt
awakes, becomes eel-like, zig-
                              zagging, diving,
          darting, glowing red eyes
in the approaching night, like a lizard's or snake's
glittering a weird warning—
and I, a two-legged predator
whose grasping hands
become an owl's hunting talons, hungry feline paws
in my desire to protect him
from the shadows and what lives in them, to bring him
into the glowing light of TV, faux grass of carpet, trimmed carrots
from dirt, air and freedom,
his sacred patch of neglect, clouds and scat—
the dog, fence frantic, barks, turns and circles
herding us both

from the other side—

Tonight, like every night
I must test his reflexes, stretch his legs, rev up his tiny heart
which pounds pathetically beneath my controlling palm
as I calm him, caught once more: smoothing ears
the colour of moonlight, whispering *Forgive us*
as I watch loosened fur settle

to the ground
like the earliest breath of winter.

Delivery Man

At age ten, he owned the six a.m. Toronto suburb
of doctors, lawyers, MPs, actuaries: winter wilderness
or vernal paradise, before the street was the street. Bearing
the day's paper burden on bony boy shoulders,
half-hunchbacked, he trudged
the sidewalk circle, bringing war, scandal, and weather
to each well-painted porch, locked door and Welcome mat. Until
   night
swallowed morning, men with cars and cells
retired kids who "really needed their sleep." So the Route Manager
   said,
dropping off his last pay, aiming a pat at disappearing
shoulders.

Now, at thirty-eight, he's back on the street,
threading downtown's maze
of profanity-spewing cars, trucks, taxis. The sunglassed
cappuccino-bearing gods of Bay Street ignore him
as he whizzes by on his old bike, backpack bulging
with the day's deliveries: fetish papers too precious
to trust to electronics, requiring assertive pen flicks
of the Cartier-suited and Gucci- shoed.
After locking his old three-speed to a parking
meter, face unshaven, in jeans and cycle clips,
he proffers packages, like a lover

to the well-sprayed and well-scraped, inside echoing
fortress foyers guarded by glass and gleam. Like serotonin,
he connects pathways, leaping gaps and dead ends
to deliver the awaited signal,
receiving robotic nods from uniformed bouncers. Sometimes he
  even rides
the elevator to move brainwork from desk to desk, flushing out
  secretaries
like startled partridge. Then, pocketing his pay,
springing the bike lock, fighting currents, he pedals back
to the silence of his room. Turns on the computer.

So, a life
lived on the threshold, the doorstep, never
stepping inside to earn a name, or leave its mark.
Except for the internet packages he sends at night, containing
  his own
midnight plans for fame:
novels delivered like time bombs to strangers online, browsing
  for porn or
procrastination. Or diatribes
against lawyers, businessmen, politicians
posted anonymously.

Bob, Flying

My brother-in-law, one of three *sons* of the *boar**
is rooted to earth with sore knees, generous belly, big
heart, quick hug, ready *How are Ya?* grin-answered (by him) *Just Fine.*
Always ready to cook up a turkey dinner
with trimmings,
or pancakes and bacon on family visits
while his wife sits alone on the screened-in porch, smoking—

Like a gnome, he knows the underneath
is well-grounded in the universal need for cables and connections
septic systems, backyard decks
and this weekend he helped us prepare a new foundation for family life:
laying pseudo-wood strips over ripped linoleum (he sat in the baby-smooth centre, after,
Buddha-content, shoes off, surrounded by bottles of *Coors Light*)—

Bob's Your Uncle is doubly reassuring with us—

But his happiest memory, he reveals over his latest dinner of steak and baked
is of flying—minus engine, wings, safety demonstrations, over-priced beer—
hooked to a parasailing craft on the day they stopped work to wait for parts,

dangling under a silken rainbow cloud
just off the coast of Turkey. Lifted above wives, wires, machinery, bills
for thirty unaccounted minutes, he drifted over
blinding blue ache of the Aegean
to see hidden inhabitants of the sea
purple jelly fish, green sea turtles
caught in tidal traffic, going about their work below
delicate innards protected by poison barbs or sharp-edged shells:
I coulda hadda heart attack—gone, a kinda Heaven.
But the wind changed; it dropped—
he lifts big hands, joined at the wrist, as if praying
or catching fastballs at the plate, sighs:
They reeled me in, like a flying fish.

**Mac/Mc—Cullach (Gaelic)*

In the Web

> "But superstition, like belief, must die,
> And remains when disbelief has gone?"
> —Philip Larkin, "Church Going"

Under towering November clouds
Angevin atheists
talk over the still small voice,
weaving conversations
on mobile-wearing walks
from boulangerie to bookstore, bank to café
under empty eyes of their fourteeth-century Virgin.

Stumbling towards the Chateau
and closing time, I push through
multilingual nets of intention, racing traffic signals:
stone leviathan, centuries-old fortress
earth-mantled by moss and pigeon nests,
guards the empty moat
that once housed Duke of Anjou's deer and antelope,
ancient paths tracing this spot
now dedicated to daily auto-pilgrimage,
Dusk comes down like a portcullis
as I cross the stone bridge
to slip seven Euros in a hand

wander the gravel walks, glimpse the river's ways
and follow the signs
to the Tapestry of the Apocalypse. Lost
in the Revolution, later found warming
haunches of royal horses, or shielding
orange trees from frost,
now hung in air-conditioned shadow
for our blind gazes to slide over
minus Kodak's crutch: flash photography
forbidden, in deference to aged dyes.
Product of seven years labour
by Bataille and de Bruges*
and an army of monks
transcendent in anonymity
who wove their faith
into stitched images of the final Uncovering,
and magnified the city of God.

Seventy-six panels, woven witness of an era
almost as hugely absurd as the dinosaurs',
in thousands of threads, silk and wool, spinning a story
we can barely remember remembering—
instead, silicon-chip knitting of computers
to modems, to cell phones, to cameras, to the web
of videoclips or soundbytes

from sages on happiness,
prophets of global warming,
the latest televised crusades
for oil and bombs, monuments and votes.
Not this Seven-headed Beast—
Nor this destruction of the City—
Not this breaking
of the Seventh Seal—

Accused by the Saint's recording quill and scroll
I buy a souvenir postcard
I cannot translate in either language,
wondering how to fill it
as I walk out into clouds of car-exhaust
today's breaths, hung on cobblestone walks
like the invisible nets of spiders
draped on moss which nibbles at the towers.
Catching the unseen drops of another day,
only these weavings will endure,
loyal not to stone, but only air

**Nicholas Bataille, master weaver. Hennequin de Bruges, painter.*

How to Look Good Naked

Despite many saleable solutions: workouts for *Better Abs,*
Tighter Buns, or *A Bikini-Body in Just Six Weeks*, there are remedies
that might not require a personal trainer, gastric bypass or
grapefruit diet:

One: Try standing in front of your dog, before
the shower, after the sweaty day: see how the pheromones fill
his nostrils, so that he sniffs with appreciation, tail lifts
like a flag announcing delighted animal sovereignty. Walks closer,
muzzle
reaching—whoa, too close!
Is it possible his beautiful nakedness is equally ignored?

Two: What about choosing to view stretch-marks, scars, sags
lines, wrinkles, valleys and flesh-dimples as mappings
of the territory, the journey so far, saying **YOU ARE HERE**?
Is it possible to be grateful for miles walked
smiles smiled, thoughts thought
for muscles used, burdens carried, even if crookedly,
so that one side slopes or leans more
than the other, like a weather-tested house? What about where
babies were made,
nine-month-nested, nursed and carried, on hip or shoulder? Where
fathers were born
in the frown lines masking uncertainty, in the stoop and softening

earned by hoisting, holding, waiting?

What about waking
to morning's slender lengthening,
 as you rise taller
like a birch bathed in midnight rain
instead of evening's locomotive of care that crashed
into the mattress,
perhaps beside another wreck,
equally well-used? What about deciding that all of this
and more, carried with you, is somehow the
tender burden you have been given, but only for a life sentence?
  And knowing
that it will all
disappear one day, that you too must wear it down
as a candle flame devours its wax foundation?

Three: What about choosing the one who loves you most (no, not you) for your mirror?

Acknowledgements

Some of these poems—or earlier versions of them—have been previously published in *Journal of the Motherhood Initiative for Research and Community Involvement (MIRCI)*, *Journal of the Association for Research on Mothering (ARM)*, *Literary Mama: Reading for the Maternally Inclined*, *Canadian Literature* and *The Windsor Review*.

"First Birds" received Honourable Mention in the 2008 "Mothers and Daughters" Poetry Contest sponsored by ARM.

I would also like to extend my appreciation to Dr. Andrea O'Reilly, "Great Mother" of MIRCI and Demeter Press Publisher, for the opportunity to put this book together—and so efficiently and pleasurably! My thanks also to Luciana Ricciutelli and Tracey Carlyle for their expert assistance with the production process.

Cover photo: courtesy of Mark Kruk

Photo: Ian McCulloch

Born and raised in the suburbs of Toronto, Laurie Kruk is currently Associate Professor of English Studies at Nipissing University in North Bay. Specializing in Canadian Literature, Kruk has published scholarly essays on Carol Shields, Timothy Findley, Joy Kogawa and others, as well as *The Voice is the Story: Conversations with Canadian Writers of Short Fiction* (2003). Her poetry has been published in over twenty literary and academic journals or anthologies, culminating in two collections. Her first collection, *Theories of the World* (1992), traces the struggle to move from (sheltered, suburban) girlhood to womanhood. Her second, *Loving the Alien* (2006), deals more explicitly with adult relationships, concluding with her initiation into the joy and struggle of mothering.